contents

This book was approved by John Legend

Photography by Danny Clinch

Piano/vocal arrangements by John Nicholas

Cherry Lane Music Company
Director of Publications/Project Editor: Mark Phillips
Manager of Publications: Gabrielle Fastman

ISBN-13: 978-1-57560-946-1
ISBN: 1-57560-946-0

Visit our website at www.cherrylane.com 

John Legend once again

In 2004 John Legend (then known primarily as an in-demand all-star studio session man) stepped into the solo spotlight as a premier singer-songwriter-pianist-performer in his own right with his debut album, *Get Lifted.* Driven in part by the hit singles "Ordinary People" and "Used to Love U," *Get Lifted* was a critical and commercial triumph, earning Legend an astounding eight Grammy nominations—he won Best New Artist, Best Male R&B Vocal Performance ("Ordinary People") and Best R&B album—and selling more than three million copies worldwide.

For most performers, achievements of that magnitude would be the culmination of a dream. For John Legend, however, awards and sales are merely fringe benefits. His real goal and gift is to tap into something honest and true within his audience and himself, and to connect on that level. When asked what he hopes his fans will glean from his much-anticipated sophomore album, he replies, "I want them to hear that I've grown; that I'm trying to take them to new places and to be excited about that. This album is an expansion more than anything else. I'm trying to be me and to embrace all the parts of me that have grown up, listened to more music, and soaked up more influences. *Get Lifted* was me then. *This* is me now."

Once Again, Legend's new album, is many things; chief among them, it's a pop/soul album fueled by intelligence, intuition, sensuality, spirit, and a creativity enhanced by Raphael Saadiq, Kanye West, Craig Street, and will.i.am, who brought the lead single, "Save Room," to Legend. Breezy and sexy, "Save Room" is a joyful, cool love song inspired by the old AM radio single "Stormy," by the Classics IV (a '60s Top 40 band best known for "Spooky"). As Legend recalls, "Will brought the sample. I didn't even know the original. I just knew it was a nice organ sound and wanted to write to it. I just started mumbling along to it, finding my place in the melody, and it worked for me."

Laced with a somewhat more dramatic flair is the mid-tempo "Where Did My Baby Go." Says Legend, "It was one of the only songs written before I began recording this album, and it was in my head for a long time. I didn't know what I was going to do with it because at the time it didn't sound like anything I'd done before. It ended up fitting perfectly because I ended up writing more stuff in that direction—so it became a precursor to where I was going this time."

Legend takes a somewhat political perspective on the stately "Coming Home," which he says is "about a soldier who wants to come back to his family, his uncertainty about being away, and whether or not he might die. It's subtle but it still manages to speak to some important issues about life and death, war and peace."

Relationship ups and downs are the subject of the swaying Kanye West—produced "Heaven Only Knows." "It's a song that just came together in a natural, effortless way, which is how Kanye and I work," Legend explains. "He played me a sample and a drum loop, and I started writing around it." Legend recorded 30 tracks, including four with Kanye, for his new album. Two of the West-produced tracks made the final track list, with West also serving as co-Executive Producer of the album. "On a creative counsel level," Legend says, "I benefit from his taste and judgment."

"Show Me," which Legend cites as one of his favorites, is hushed, haunting, and deliberately ambiguous. Co-produced by Raphael Saadiq and Craig Street (Me'Shell NdegéOcello, Cassandra Wilson), "Show Me" was, according to Legend, "intended to be about God, but I wanted it to have the feel of a romantic song as well. But while I could have done what I usually do and write about a relationship, this felt like such a spiritual song. I've never sung or recorded my voice like that. When I'm with a girl and I have a song in my head, I kind of whisper it in her ear, like an intimate whisper. That's how I did the vocal for this song."

Even more so *than* he did on *Get Lifted*, Legend went boldly in his own creative direction on *Once Again*, opting to write not from a marketing standpoint, but from his heart and soul and personal experience. "I listen to a lot of music," he says about the preparation for the album. "The producers I work with—like Kanye, Will, and Craig—listen to a lot more, and we just brainstorm and don't limit it to 'what's going on in urban music right now.' I didn't want to put a box around it. You make music, try to make it as good as you possibly can, trust the people around you, and hope and pray that what you really love is something a lot of other people will also love. With *Get Lifted*, we managed to make a strong record that people related to. We succeeded because it was distinctive and it touched a chord. So I figured, 'Let me just keep making music that's really good and that touches people—music that they can feel, which has some beauty to it and that transcends what the marketers are going to tell you—and we'll figure out a way to get it to people.'"

John Legend (nee Stephens) grew up in Ohio, surrounded by every musical influence from gospel to hip-hop. While attending the University of Pennsylvania (where he majored in English), Legend found time to make his own music, whether it was recording his own albums, performing at talent shows and open mics, or directing the choir at a local church. In fact, just months before he began work on *Get Lifted*, he finally ended a nine-year tenure as music and choir director at Bethel A.M.E. Church in northeastern Pennsylvania.

In 1998, Legend got his first taste of success, playing piano on "Everything Is Everything," from Lauryn Hill's multiple Grammy-winning album, *The Miseducation of Lauryn Hill*. He also honed his chops touring throughout the East Coast, opening for bigger R&B acts and recording and selling several live concert albums. In 2001 a college roommate introduced Legend to the then up-and-coming producer/artist Kanye West. By 2002 Legend was part of West's creative team, appearing on albums by Talib Kweli, Common, and Mary J. Blige, as well as on West's 2004 breakthrough, *The College Dropout*. That same year Legend lent his vocal talent to Alicia Keys' "You Don't Know My Name" and appeared on Jay-Z's acclaimed *Black Album*.

In late 2003 Legend became the first artist signed to Kanye's KonMan Entertainment (later renamed Getting Out Our Dreams), and a deal with Columbia Records followed in May 2004. Preloaded with pre-release buzz, *Get Lifted* debuted at #7 on the *Billboard* Top 200 and #1 on the R&B Album chart the week of its release, three days after Christmas 2004.

Three years ago, John Legend was a highly regarded session musician. Today he's an artist who proves that, even in an age of expediency and crass commercialism, real talent not only still matters but will be acknowledged. When asked how success has affected him, Legend replies, "I think I'm happier, not just because of winning Grammys and selling records, but because it's really fulfilling to have all these things happen with something you love to do. Seeing my music elevated and receiving an almost universally positive response to that music makes me feel better every day. I feel more confident and inspired, and that's fun. I'm feeling truly creative, and I hope that feeling will stay around—because my hope and belief is that most people are down to grow and explore with me."

Save Room

Words and Music by
John Stephens, Will Adams, Jessyca Wilson,
Buddy Buie and James Cobb Jr.

Am9
5fr
love is worth a mo - ment of your time.
pain; pleas - ure is on the oth - er side.
Knock - ing on your door
Let down your guard
Make time to live
Gmaj9
Am9
Gmaj9
just a lit - tle.
just a lit - tle.
a lit - tle.
So cold out - side to - night.
I'll keep you safe in these arms of mine.
Don't let this mo - ment slip by to - night.
Am9
Gmaj9
Let's get a fi - re burn - ing. Oh, I
Hold on to me. Pret - ty ba - by, you will
You nev - er know what you're miss - ing till you
C
know I'll keep it burn - ing bright
see I can be all you need
try. I'll keep you sat - is - fied
if you stay.

Bm
B
Am9
5fr
Won't you stay, stay? Save room for my love.
cresc.
f
mf
Gmaj7
2fr
Am9
5fr
Gmaj7
2fr
Save room for a mo - ment to be with me.
Am9
5fr
Gmaj7
2fr
C
Save room for my love. Save a lit - tle, save a lit - tle for me.
Bm
B
To Coda
Won't you save a lit - tle, save a lit - tle for me, oh.

Am9
5fr
Gmaj9
5fr
Am9
5fr
(Pa ya pa pa,
pa ya pa pa,
Gmaj9
5fr
Am9
5fr
Gmaj9
5fr
pa ya pa pa
da da
C
D.S. al Coda
da.)
Oh,
come on.
1.2.
3.
D.S.S. and fade
Coda
Bm
B
B

Heaven

Words and Music by
John Stephens, Kayne West, Milton Bland,
Alexandra Louise Brown, Jessyca Wilson
and Vaughn Stephens

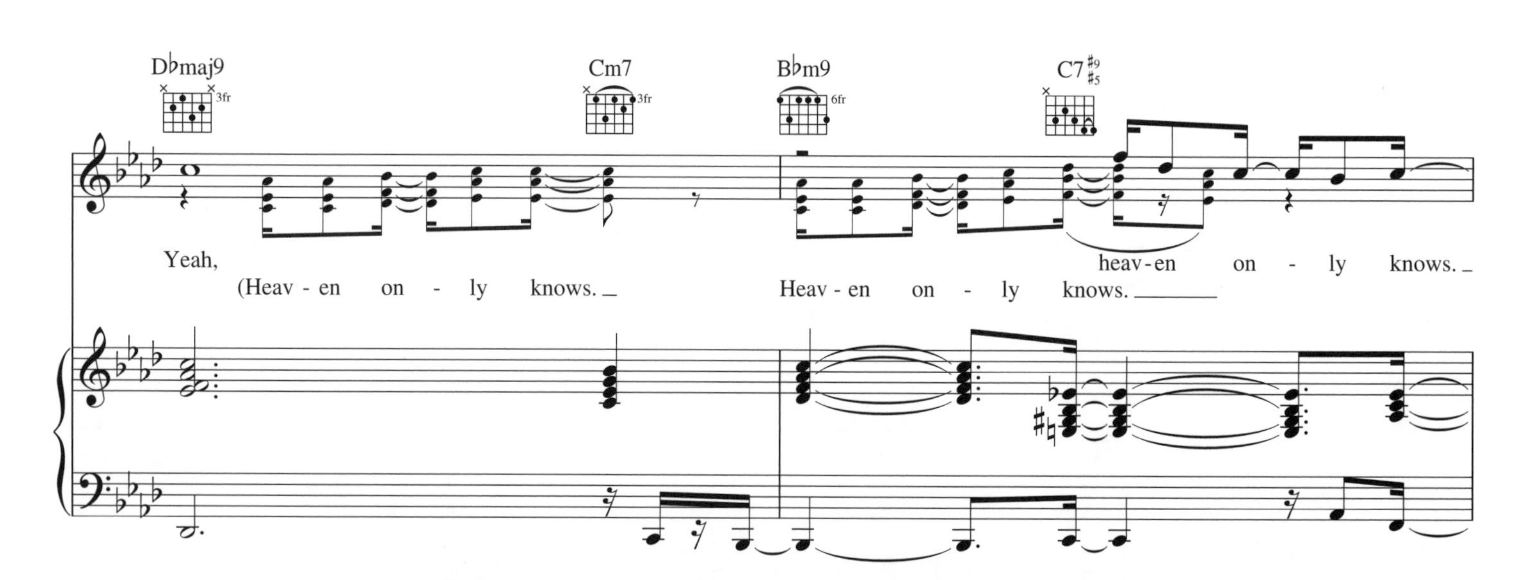

Fm7
Em7
E♭m7
A♭9
Oh,
heav-en on - ly knows.
Heav-en on - ly knows.
Heav-en on - ly knows.
D♭maj9
Cm7
B♭m9
C7♯9♯5
Oh,
heav-en on - ly knows.
Heav-en on - ly knows.
Heav-en on - ly knows.
Fm7
Em7
E♭m7
A♭9
Yeah.
Heav - en on - ly knows.
Heav-en on - ly knows.)

D♭maj9
B♭m9
C7♯9♯5
Fm7
Last night was the worst night, be - gin - ning of the end. Or
Make this night the best night. It's time for a sec - ond chance.
Em7
E♭m7
A♭9
may - be it be - gan be - fore, and here we go a - gain.
Turn the beat up on re - peat and we could start to dance.
D♭maj9
B♭m9
C7♯9♯5
Fm7
Things got so dra - mat - ic; things got out of hand.
Some - times when we're talk - ing, words get drowned out by the sound. So

Em7
E♭m7
A♭9
We said words we could - n't i - mag - ine, and I don't un - der - stand. Oh,
let's get back to touch - ing; we'll get back on sol - id ground. Oh,
D♭maj9
3fr
B♭m9
6fr
C7♯9♯5
Fm7
3fr
3
there you go with the same old thing. When
let's hold hands, like the young ro - mance.
Em7
E♭m7
A♭9
things go wrong, oh, you al - ways seem to blame me. Well,
Let's first kiss like the mo - ment we first did.

D♭maj9
B♭m9
C7♯9♯5
Fm7
now I'd like to find what se - crets hide in your mind,
Can we make love like way back in the day, love?
Em7
E♭m7
A♭9
where the end will go, will I nev - er know?
We could lose con - trol; ba - by, don't say no.
Heav-en on - ly knows.
D♭maj9
B♭m9
C7♯9♯5
Fm7
Heav-en on - ly knows.
(Heav - en on - ly knows. Heav - en on - ly knows.

Em7
E♭m7
A♭9
Heav - en on - ly knows.
Heav - en on - ly knows.
Heav - en on - ly knows.
D♭maj9
B♭m9
C7♯9♯5
Fm7
Heav - en on - ly knows.
Heav - en on - ly knows.
Heav - en on - ly knows.
1.
Em7
E♭m7
A♭9
Yeah.
Heav - en on - ly knows.
Heav - en on - ly knows.)

2.
A♭9
D♭maj9
Cm7
B♭m9
Yeah,
Heav-en on-ly knows.
Will you come back to me?
C7♯9♯5
Fm7
Em7
E♭m7
heav-en on-ly knows.
Oh,
Will you run back to me?
Will you come back to me?
A♭9
D♭maj9
Cm7
B♭m9
heav-en on-ly knows.
Oh,
Will you run back to me?
Will you come back to me?

C7♯9♯5
Fm7
3fr
Em7
E♭m7
oh,
yeah.
Oh,
oh,
Will you run back to me?
Will you come back to me?
A♭9
D♭maj9
3fr
Will you run back to me?)
Make this night the best night. It's
B♭m9
6fr
C7♯9♯5
Fm7
3fr
Em7
E♭m7
time for a sec-ond chance.
Turn the beat up on re-peat and
A♭9
D♭maj9
3fr
we could start to dance.
Oh... (Heav-en on-ly knows.

B♭m9
C7#9#5
Fm7
Em7
E♭m7
Heav-en on-ly knows.
Heav-en on-ly knows.
A♭9
D♭maj9
B♭m9
Heav-en on-ly knows.
Heav-en on-ly knows.
C7#9#5
Fm7
Em7
E♭m7
Heav-en on-ly knows.
(Heav-en on-ly knows.
1.
2.
A♭9
A♭9
D♭5
Heav-en on-ly knows.)
Heav-en on-ly knows.)

Stereo

Words and Music by
John Stephens, Tom Craskey
and Devon Harris

Fm
She's a
fast love pro - fes - sion - al,
Turn on the vid - e - o.

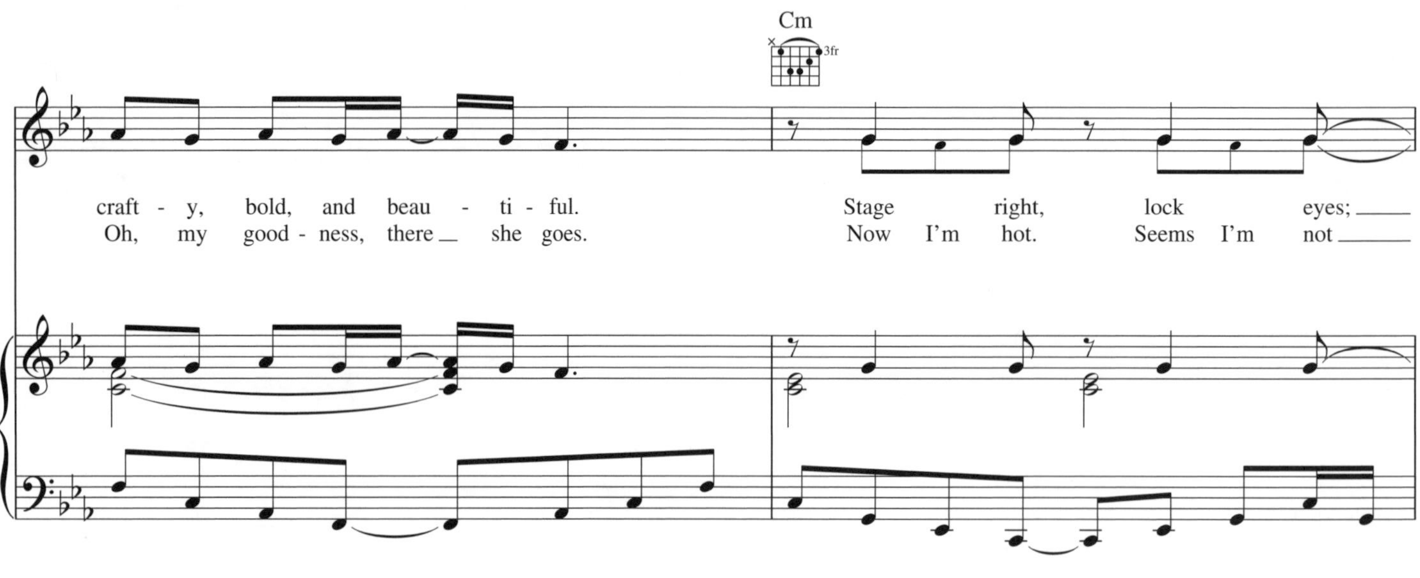
Cm
3fr
craft - y, bold, and beau - ti - ful.
Oh, my good - ness, there she goes.
Stage right, lock eyes;
Now I'm hot. Seems I'm not

Fm
I swear it's mag - i - cal.
the on - ly one she knows.
Her name is Mel - a - nie.
Name - drop - ping ev - 'ry day, but

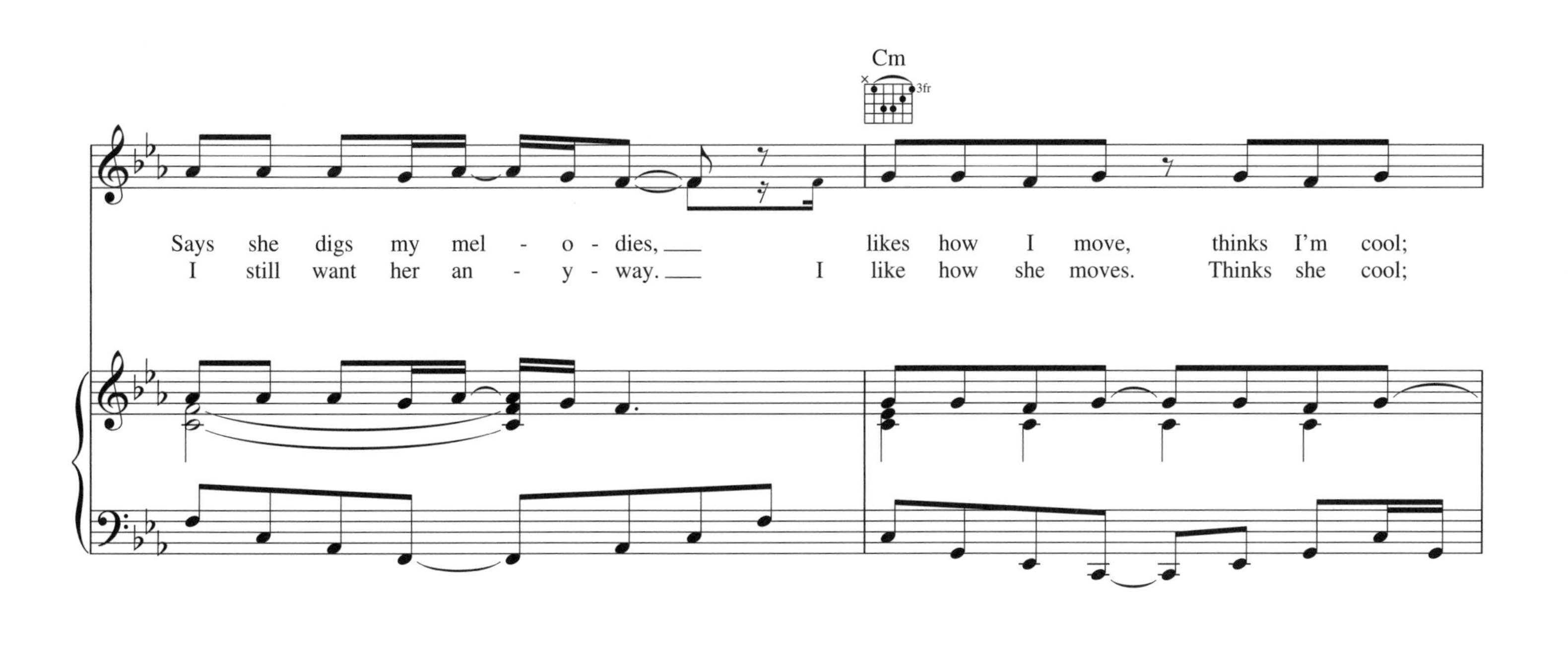
Cm
Says she digs my mel - o - dies, likes how I move, thinks I'm cool;
I still want her an - y - way. I like how she moves. Thinks she cool;

Fm
that's what she says to me. Big stage, bright lights.
my fa - v'rite get - a - way. Big stage, bright lights.

Cm
Short love, long nights. Fre - quent flights through the skies to see stars. I come
Short love, long nights. Dé - jà vu, yeah, we do it a - gain. Off to

Fm
back to town, she's hang - ing a - round. It still
the next town, she's on to the next round. Let it go.
Cm
feels so real, but we can't go too far.
We both know that it's all gon - na end.
Fm
Her fa - v'rite col - ors be plat - 'num 'n' gold. She
Cm
on - ly loves in ster - e - o. She on - ly loves in ster - e - o.

Fm
I should know 'cause I've seen it be - fore. I
Cm
To Coda
think I got - ta let her go. She on - ly loves in ster - e - o. Oh,
Fm
Cm
oh, oh, oh, oh, oh.
1.
2.
Fm
Oh, oh, oh,

Cm
oh,
oh,
oh.
A♭
Fm
She fell in love with the ra - di - o.
It
Dm7♭5
G
was - n't real - ly me,
so I had to let her go.
Just ask
A♭
Fm
an - y D - J back in her home - town,
she

D.S. al Coda
Dm7♭5
Cm
3fr
likes to get a - round.
Just watch as she gets down.
Oh, oh.
Coda
Fm
oh, oh, oh.
She loves in ster -
1.2.3.
Cm
e - o.
Oh,
4.
Cm
e - o, oh, oh, oh, oh, oh.

Show Me

Words and Music by
John Stephens, Estelle Swaray
and Raphael Saadiq

D
B♭
I real - ized as I lay down to sleep,
Guess it's fun - ny how I say thanks to you
F
C
we have - n't spoke in weeks.
for all you're giv - en me.
D
B♭
So man - y things that I'd like to know.
Some - times the price of what you gave to me,
F
C
Come have a talk with me.
I can't stop ques - tion - ing.

D
Bb
I need a sign, some - thing I can see.
O, God of love, peace, and mer - cy,
6
F
C
Why all the mys - ter - y?
why so much suf - fer - ing?
D
Bb
I try not to fall for make - be - lieve,
I pray for the world; it gets worse to me.
F
A7
but what is re - al - i - ty?
Won - der if you're lis - ten - ing.

Bb
F
Where do we go? What do we know?
When peo - ple go, why do they go?
May - be we'll talk some oth - er night.
C
G
Life has to have a mean - ing.
Why don't you choose me? But
Right now I'll take it eas - y.
Bb
F
Show me the light. Show me the way.
some - day I know I'm gon - na go.
Won't spend my time wait - ing to die;

C
G
Show that you're lis - ten - ing.
I hope you're wait - ing for me.
en - joy the life I'm liv - ing.
Chorus
D
B♭
Show me that you love me.
F
C
Show me that you walk with me.
D
B♭
Hope - ful - ly, just a - bove me,

1.
F
C
heav - en's watch - ing o - ver me.
2.
D
B♭
F
C
D
B♭
D.S. and fade on Chorus
F
A7

Each Day Gets Better

Words and Music by
John Stephens, Will Adams,
Pamela Sawyer and Frank Wilson

F
E♭maj7
Dm7
I just can't let her go,
oh no.
Cm7
3fr
To Coda I
F
To Coda II
Each kiss gets sweet - er.
I just can't leave her, no.
E♭maj7
Dm7
I'll write a song.
She wants to breathe.
Cm7
3fr
F
I thought a - bout it for far too long.
She wants to be where the grass is green.

E♭maj7
Dm7
But I've never had someone to sing about
She wants to know how love's supposed to be.
Cm7
F
until I met her. Now each day gets better.
She wants it better. I want to let her
E♭maj7
Dm7
Nobody knows, nobody sees,
know she belongs right here with me.
Cm7
F
nobody else understands me like she.
She's heard it all, but I'll make her see.

E♭maj7
Dm7
3
Now that I know (what) true love means,
I'll make her fall, make her be - lieve. I'll
1.
Cm7
3fr
E♭/F
I just hope she stays with me.
Where do we go?
2.
Cm7
F
D.S. al Coda I
prom - ise her that I'll nev - er leave.
And where do we go?
Coda I
F
E♭maj7
Dm7
I just can't leave her, no.
Oh, no.

Cm7
3fr
F
F7sus4
Each kiss gets sweet - er.
I just can't leave her, no.
A♭13
G7
I just had to write a song a - bout her.
Cm7
3fr
A♭7
4fr
Tell her I don't want to live with - out her.
D7♯9
4fr
G7
Tell her I would build my world a - round her,

Cm7
3fr
A♭7
4fr
deep - er and deep - er, sweet - er and sweet - er.
E♭/F
F
D.S. al Coda II
I'll nev - er leave her a - lone.
Where do we go?
Coda II
E♭maj7
Dm7
Cm7
3fr
F
Repeat and fade
Each day gets bet - ter. I just can't let her go.
Each kiss gets sweet - er. I just can't leave her, no.

PDA
(We Just Don't Care)

Words and Music by
John Stephens, Jessyca Wilson,
Eric Hudson and Kawan Prather

*Recorded a half step lower.

Cmaj7
Fmaj7
Cmaj7
Bm7♭5
neath the stars.
May - be we'll go too far.
We just don't care.
E7
We just don't care.
We just don't care.
Fmaj7
Cmaj7
You know I love it when you're lov - ing me.
I see you're clos - ing down the res - tau - rant.
Fmaj7
Cmaj7
Some - times it's bet - ter when it's pub - lic - ly.
Let's sneak and do it when your boss is gone.

Fmaj7
Cmaj7
Bm7♭5
I'm not a - shamed; I don't care who sees us hug -
Ev - 'ry - bod - y's leav - ing; we'll have some fun. Oh, may -
E7
ging and kiss - ing; a love ex - hi - bi - tion, oh.
be it's wrong, but you're turn - ing me on, oh.
Fmaj7
Cmaj7
We'll ren - dez - vous out in the fire es - cape.
We'll take a vis - it to your ma - ma's house,
Fmaj7
Cmaj7
I'd like to set off an a - larm to - day,
creep to the bed - room while your ma - ma's out.

Fmaj7
Cmaj7
Bm7♭5
a love e - mer - gen - cy. Don't make me wait. Just fol -
May - be she'll hear it when we scream and shout, but we'll
E7
low, I'll lead you. I ur - gent - ly need you, oh.
keep it rock - in' un - til she comes knock - in', oh.
𝄋
Fmaj7
Cmaj7
Fmaj7
Let's go to the park. I wan - na kiss you un - der -
Cmaj7
Fmaj7
Cmaj7
Bm7♭5
neath the stars. May - be we'll go too far. We just don't care.

E7
We just don't care. We just don't...
Fmaj7
Cmaj7
Let's make love.
Fmaj7
Cmaj7
Let's go some - where they might dis - cov - er us.
Fmaj7
Cmaj7
Bm7♭5
Let's get lost in lust. We just don't care.

E7
1.
We just don't care. We just don't care.
2.
Fmaj7
We just don't care. If we keep up all this fool-
Em7
Ebm7
Dm7
G7
Cmaj7
ing a-round, we'll be the talk of the town.
Cm7
3fr
F7
Bbmaj7
F/G
I'll tell the world of our love an-y-time. Let's o-

G7
pen the blinds, 'cause we real - ly don't mind.
Fmaj7
Cmaj7
Fmaj7
Cmaj7
Fmaj7
Cmaj7
Bm7♭5
E7

Fmaj7
Cmaj7
Oh, I don't care a - bout pro - pri - e - ty.
Fmaj7
Cmaj7
Let's break the rules, ig - nore so - ci - e - ty.
Fmaj7
Cmaj7
Bm7♭5
May - be our neigh - bors like to spy, it's true, so what
E7
D.S. and fade
if they watch when we do what we do, oh.

Slow Dance

Words and Music by
John Stephens, Will Adams,
Estelle Swaray and Lewis Poindexter

talk - ing loud, you're wild - ing out. Don't seem like my old la - dy.
pol - i - tics and talk - ing shit ain't real - ly none of my bus' - ness.
Let's go and play the songs we used to play. Can we
Let's go and play the songs we used to play on that
re - ig - nite the flame, 'cause things just ain't the same? We could
old school ra - di - o. Let the mu - sic soothe your soul. For -
B♭
Cm7
3fr
talk a - bout de - bat - ing. We could talk un - til we're cra - zy. We could
get a - bout the world. I'm groov - ing with my girl. For -
3
3

Gm
3fr
Cm7
3fr
fo - cus on it now, or we could fo - cus on it lat - er. We could
get a - bout the news. Slip on our danc - ing shoes. Let's not
B♭
Cm7
3fr
start an - oth - er fight. We could ar - gue and fuss all night. But I pro -
talk a - bout the war. Don't know what they're fight - ing for. I pro -
Gm
3fr
Cm7
3fr
pose
pose
that we go to the floor and we slow
B♭
Cm7
3fr
dance. To - night I wan - na dance.
(Da, da da, da.

Gm
Cm7
Can you do that with your man? Yeah.
Na, na na, na, hoo.
B♭
Cm7
Da, da, da, da.
To-night I wan-na groove
Gm
Cm7
and let the mu-sic make you move,
Na, na, na, na, hoo.
B♭
Cm7
move, move, yeah.
Da, da, da, da.

To Coda
1.
2.
Gm
Cm7
3fr
Yeah, yeah, yeah, yeah.
Woo,
Na, na, na, na, hoo.)
na, hoo.)
B♭
N.C.
hoo.
Woo,
woo,
yeah.
Yeah, I say...
I love it.
I love it.
I love it. We're slow danc - ing to - geth - er.
Play 3 times
I love it.

Cm7
Gm
Tacet
D.S. al Coda
I love it. I pro - pose that we go to the floor and we slow
Coda
Cm7
Bb
Woo, hoo. Yeah,
na, hoo. Da, da, da,
Cm7
Gm
yeah, yeah, yeah.
da. Na, na, na,
Cm7
Bb
woo, hoo.
na, hoo.)

Again

Words and Music by
John Stephens

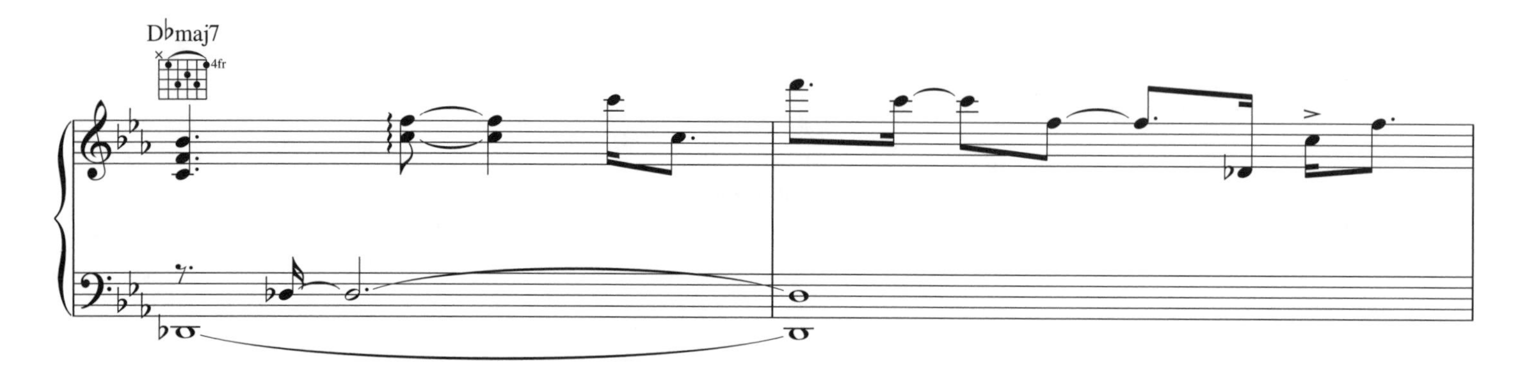

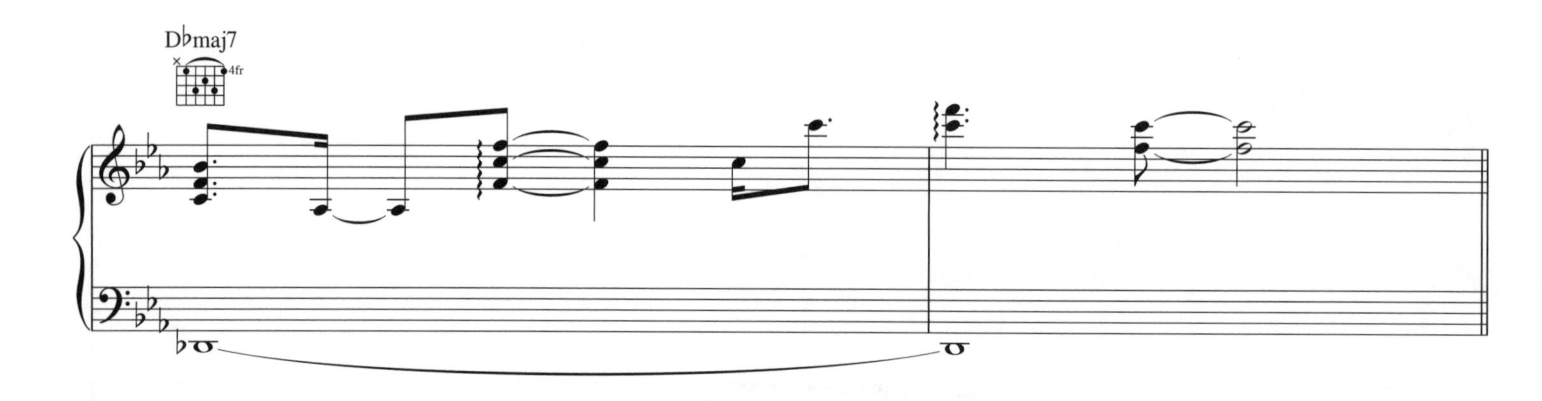

E♭maj7
6fr
First time we ev - er got a chance to be ___ a - lone, we ___ knew ___ it was wrong ___
mf
D♭maj7
4fr
___ to do. Guess that's why ___ I was drawn to you. The
E♭maj7
6fr
sec - ond time leads to the third, the fifth, ___ the sev - enth time; ___ I feel so ___
D♭maj7
4fr
___ a - live. It ___ won't last, ___ but it's ___ al - right. ___

E♭maj7
6fr
Fleet - ing joy and fad - ing ec - sta - sy. Here it goes
D♭maj7
4fr
a - gain, oh.
E♭maj7
6fr
Sneak - ing fruit from the for - bid - den free. Sweet taste
D♭maj7
4fr
Am7♭5
4fr
A♭maj7
4fr
of sin. And I'm do - in' it a - gain.

Am7♭5
A♭maj7
4fr
Yes, I'm do - in' it a - gain.
Yes, we're do - in' it a - gain.
Oh, I'm do - in' it a - gain.
Oh, we're do - in' it a - gain.
Gm7
Fm7
E♭maj7
D♭maj7
3fr
6fr
I
We
said it would end,
but here it goes
a - gain.

E♭maj7
6fr
This time you told me you saw me at the same mo - tel. You said you knew
Each time you call me home in a sweet re - frain, say - ing things -
D♭maj7
4fr
me well and I had that fa - mil - iar smell, and asked me,
'll change. You'll take a - way the pain. Then we
E♭maj7
6fr
"How am I ev - er gon - na learn to put my trust in you like you want
flash - back to the first time you put your spell on me. You en - vel -
D♭maj7
4fr
me to? 'Cause I know what you're prone to do."
op me. You feel good as hell to me.

E♭maj7
6fr
Ac - cu - sa - tions fly like bul - lets do.
Here it goes
One mo - ment leads to an - oth - er few.
Here it goes
D♭maj7
4fr
a - gain, oh.
Oh,
a - gain, oh.
Oh,
E♭maj7
6fr
you know me be - cause you're do - in' it, too.
The cy - cle nev -
leav - ing you is, oh, so hard to do.
I just can't
D♭maj7
4fr
Am7♭5
4fr
A♭maj7
4fr
er ends, it nev - er ends.
Oh, you're do - in' it a - gain.
pre - tend. I can't pre - tend.
I keep do - in' it a - gain.

Am7♭5
A♭maj7
Yes, you're do - in' it a - gain.
Oh, I'm do - in' it a - gain.
To Coda
Am7♭5
A♭maj7
Oh, you're do - in' it a - gain.
Yes, I'm do - in' it a - gain.
Gm7
Fm7
E♭maj7
D♭maj7
You said it would end, but here it goes
Emaj9
E♭maj9
a - gain and a - gain and a - gain.

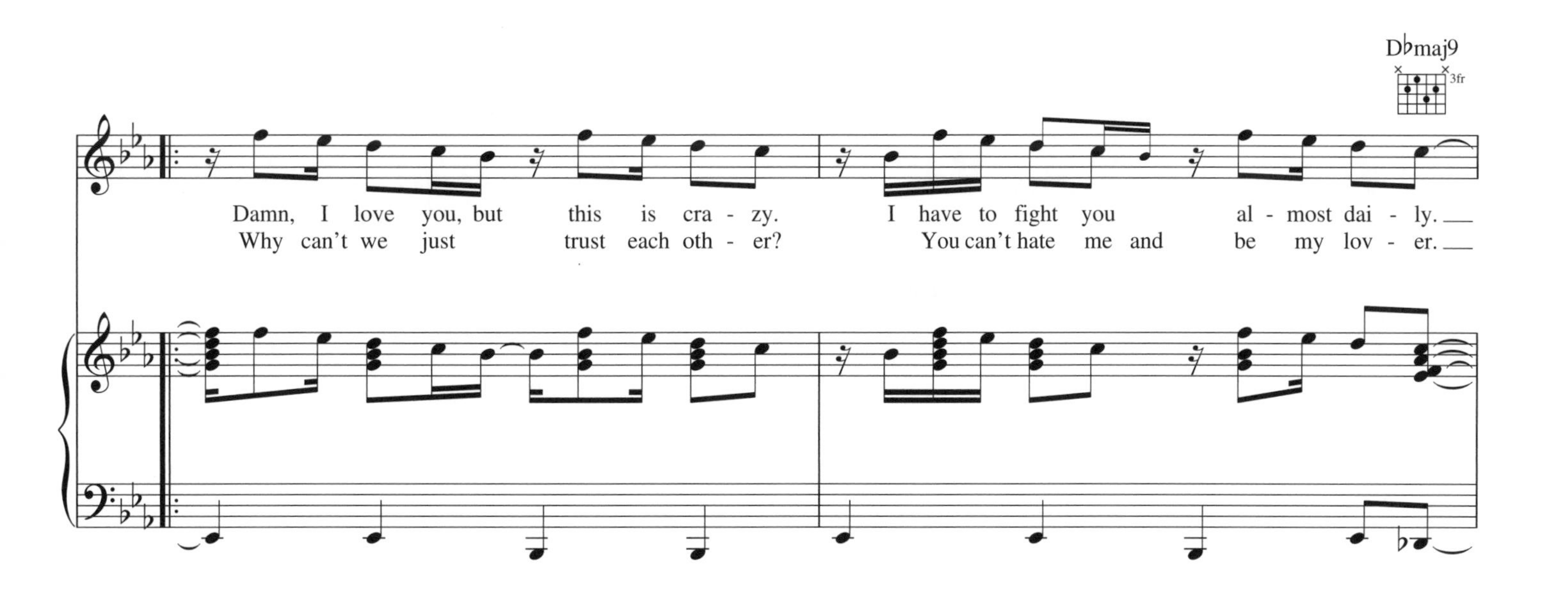
D♭maj9
3fr
Damn, I love you, but this is cra - zy. I have to fight you al - most dai - ly.
Why can't we just trust each oth - er? You can't hate me and be my lov - er.

1.
E♭maj9
5fr
We break up so fast and we, we make up so pas - sion-ate - ly.
Pas - sion ends; the pain be - gins.

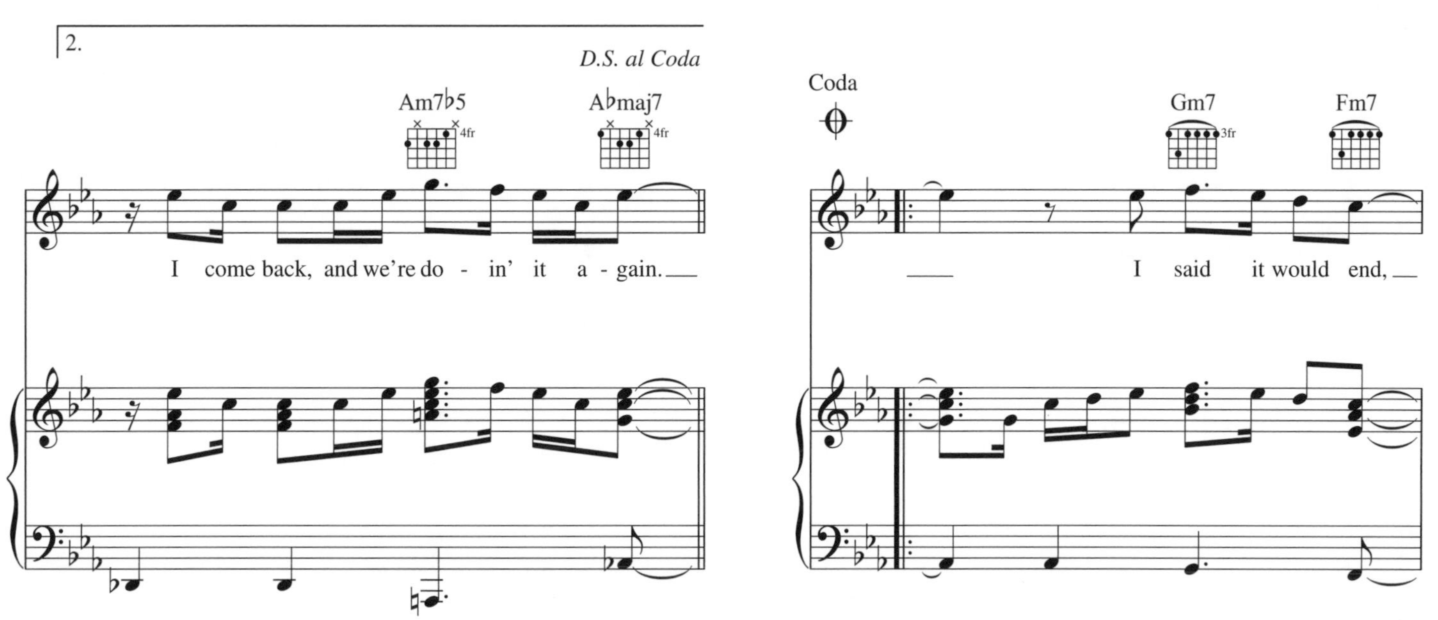
2.
D.S. al Coda
Am7♭5
4fr
A♭maj7
4fr
I come back, and we're do - in' it a - gain.
Coda
Gm7
3fr
Fm7
I said it would end,

E♭maj7
D♭maj7
oh, oh, oh, oh,
yeah.
1.
Am7♭5
A♭maj7
Oh, I'm do - in' it a - gain.
2.
Am7♭5
A♭maj7
Oh, I'm do - in' it a - gain.
Gm7
Fm7
E♭maj7
D♭maj7
I said it would end, but here it goes
Cadd2
a - gain, a - gain.
rit.

Maxine

Words and Music by
John Stephens, Om'mas Keith,
Shafiq Husayn and Taz Arnold

Am9
D13♭9
Gmaj13
but she looks just like you.
She may not be you,
but she looks just
To Coda II
Am7
like you.
(1.) You should - 've seen the way she wore
seen her eyes, her lips,
(3.) Oh, you should - 've seen the way he stroked
D7♭9
A♭7
Gmaj7
Em9
her dress and her white sti - let - to shoes.
her face. She looked as sweet as hon - ey - dew.
her hair and the smile that lit her face.
You should - 've
You should - 've
You should - 've

Am7
D7♭9
4fr
Gmaj7
seen the way they looked on her, just like the ones that I bought you.
seen the way she walked a-way. Oh, she swayed her hips like you.
seen the way he kissed her lips. Did it have the same sweet taste?
B♭maj7
I searched for days on end to no a-vail till I
I was on-ly sev-'ral steps from her, but she
Though my mind, it might be run-ning wild in
Gmaj7
B♭maj7
found them in Pe-ru. She must-'ve been to Li-ma just
nev-er no-ticed me. I took an-oth-er sip of fine
con-stant search of you, it's fun-ny how my eyes keep see-ing things
To Coda I
1.
Am7
D7♭9
4fr
as well, be-cause she had them, too. You should-'ve
li-queur. It was quite a sight to see.
my heart would not be-lieve are true.

2.
D.S. al Coda I
D7♭9
4fr
I
Coda I
D7♭9
4fr
D.S. al Coda II
I
Coda II
Fmaj7
Max - ine,
she looks just
Gmaj7
like you.
Fmaj7
Max - ine.
(You should -'ve
Gmaj7
Repeat and fade
seen her, seen her.
Max - ine.
You should -'ve
seen her, seen her.)

Where Did My Baby Go

Words and Music by
John Stephens

E7
Am7
D7sus4
D
1.2. I'm call - ing but I can't get through.
3.4. Just what am I sup - posed to do?
Bm7♭5/F
E7
Am7
Please tell that girl if you meet her that some - one's
F9
Gadd2
E7
long - ing to see her. Where did my ba - by go? I wish that she would
Play 1st time only
Am7
C/D
get back soon, get back soon.

Play 2nd, 3rd & 4th times only
F9
G
To Coda II
get back soon.
To Coda I
Em7
G
Em7
I'm
G
Em7
search - ing for the lov - er I knew.
May - be I was wrong and I ig -
G
Em7
Am7
Have you seen her? Where did she go? Feels like I've just
nored her for too long and I did - n't e - ven no - tice

C/D
G
Em7
lost my on - ly friend.
when she slipped a - way.
G
Em7
G
Flames sub - sid - ed, col - ors fad - ed. Love just got so
May - be while I lay fast a - sleep, then out in - to the
Em7
Am7
C/D
com - pli - cat - ed. Wish that I could see her smile a - gain.
night she creeps. I'll leave the light on so she'll come back some - day.
G
Em7
So if you
Oh, if you

Bm7♭5/F
E7
see her out there, tell her
see her out there, tell her
Am7
C/D
Bm7♭5/F
E7
I'm still here waiting for the day
it's not fair, and that life's just not
1.
Am7
C/D
when she will re-ap-pear.
2.
D.S. al Coda I
Am7
D
Dsus4
D
the same when she's not here.

Coda I
Em7
G
Get back soon.
Em7
G
Em7
Get back soon.
Oh,
Bm7♭5/F
Em7
Am7
C/D
oh,

Bm7♭5/F
E7
Am7
C/D
oh.
D.S. al Coda II
Coda II
Em7
Get back soon.
G
Em7
Get back soon.
G
Em7
Gmaj9
Get back soon.
rit.

Maxine's Interlude

Words and Music by
John Stephens and Dave Tozer

Amaj9
now?
Oh,
get
back
soon.
Bm7
B♭maj7
(Max
-
ine.)
Oh,
where
are
you
Amaj9
now?
(Max
-
ine.)
Oh,
get
back
soon.
B7sus2
B7
B7sus4
2fr
B7
E
Esus4/2
Where
are
you
now?

E
A/E
G♯m/A
4fr
A
Where are you now?
Whoo.
Bm7
B♭maj7
Some - times I won - der why she
Amaj9
Bm7
would - n't stay,
what I should have changed.
B♭maj7
Amaj9
Some-times I won - der why it's been so long.
What did I do wrong?

Bm7
B♭maj7
Amaj9
Max - ine, oh, Max - ine.
B7sus2
B7
B7sus4
2fr
B7
Whoo. Oh, where are you
(Where are you now?)
E
Esus4 2
E
A/E
G♯m/A
4fr
now? Oh, where are you now?
(Where are you now? Whoo.)
A
G♯m/A
4fr
A
Max - ine.

Another Again

Words and Music by
John Stephens, Kanye West,
George Patterson and Jessyca Wilson

*Recorded a half step lower.

Cmaj9
It's so dra-mat-ic a-gain. Af-ter we go at it, we get mad, then we go at it a-gain.
I can't in-vite her a-gain 'cause she'll go from a lov-er to a fight-er and I'll fight her a-gain.
Gadd9/B
G/B
Oh, I love it, then I hate it. She's my fa-v'rite a-
So, it's o-ver, but I told her to come o-ver a-
gain. I'm wast-ing time. I can't help it, she's so fine. Oh, I
gain. I'm wast-ing time, but she's al-ways on my mind. I can't
like her style, and I love the way she talks and I smile.
let her go. Oh, she's not the best, but she's all that I know.

Cmaj9
As much as we may try, can't quite see eye

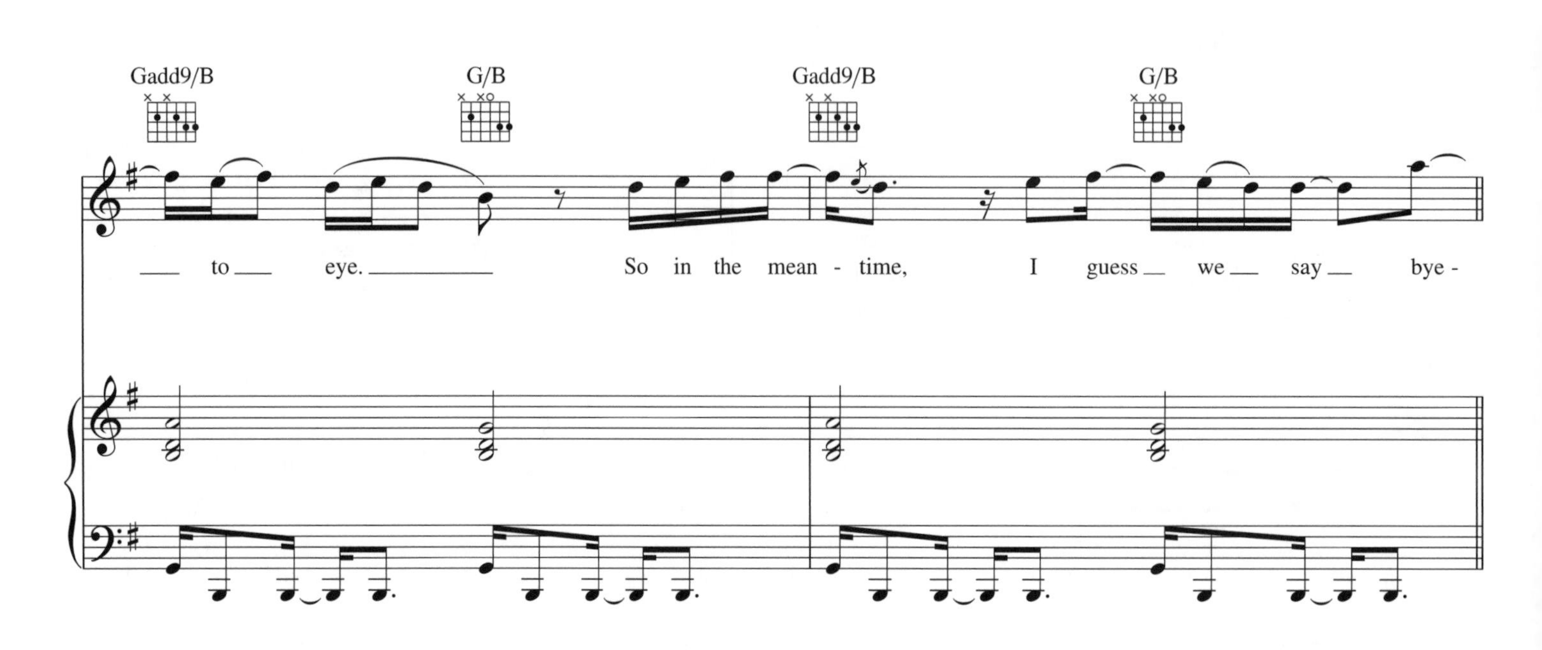
Gadd9/B
G/B
Gadd9/B
G/B
to eye.
So in the mean - time,
I guess we say bye -

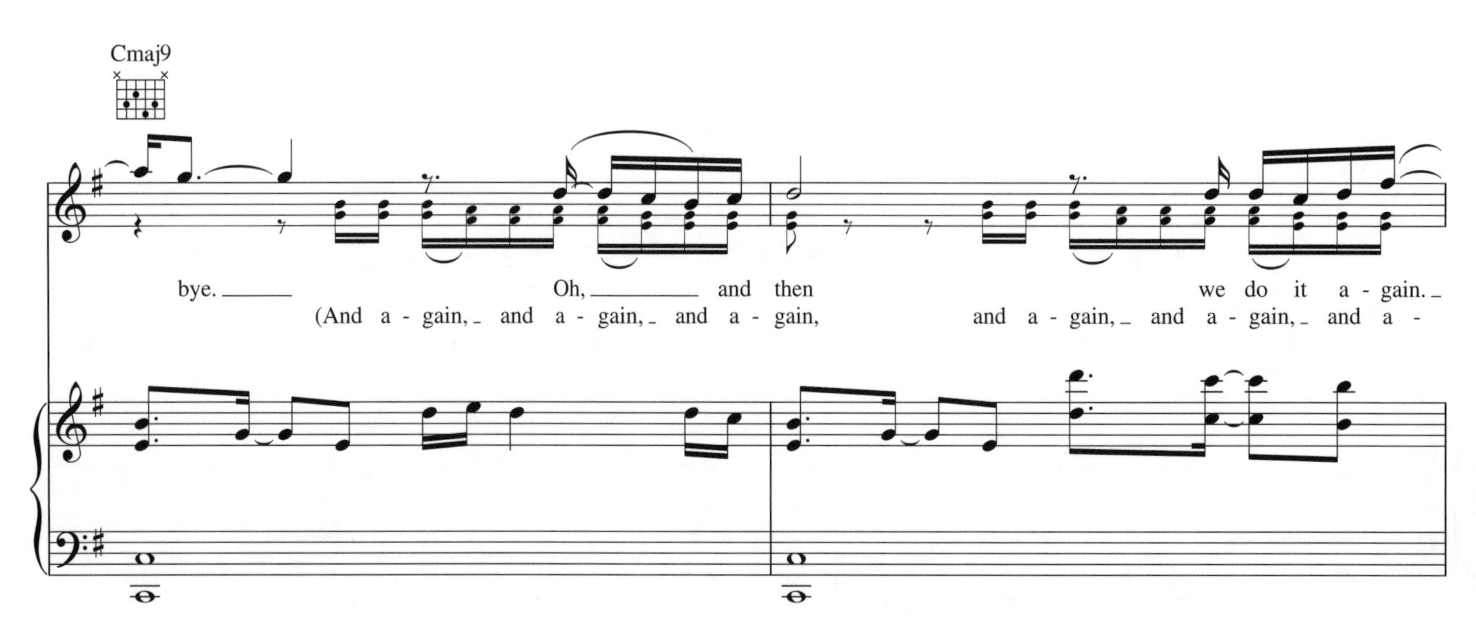
Cmaj9
bye. Oh, and then we do it a - gain.
(And a - gain, and a - gain, and a - gain, and a - gain, and a - gain, and a -

Gadd9/B
G/B
Gadd9/B
G/B
We do it a - gain, and we do it a - gain.
gain.

Cmaj9
Oh, and then we do it a - gain.
And a - gain, and a - gain, and a - gain, and a - gain, and a - gain, and a -

Gadd9/B
G/B
Gadd9/B
G/B
We want it a - gain, and we want it a - gain.
gain.)

Cmaj9
Gadd9/B
G/B
Gadd9/B
G/B
Cmaj9
So I've got a new friend. I wish I could for - get you, but I miss you, wan - na kiss you a -
3
Gadd9/B
G/B
Gadd9/B
G/B
gain. Oh, she's like you, but she's not you. Got - ta find you a - gain.

Cmaj9
So we re-mem-ber a-gain, the mid-dle of De-cem-ber and I took you out to din-ner a-gain.
Gadd9/B
G/B
Oh, I love her. It's not o - ver. Just an-oth - er a-gain.
Oh, an-oth - er a-gain,
(And a-gain, and a-gain, and a-gain, and a-gain, and a-gain, and a - gain.)
Repeat and fade
an-oth - er, it's an-oth - er a-gain.

Coming Home

Words and Music by
John Stephens and Will Adams

B♭
F/A
know that life took us a - part, but you're still with - in my heart.
An - oth - er sol - dier gone to war, an - oth - er sto - ry told be - fore.
G7
B♭/C
I go to sleep and feel your spir - it next to me.
Now it's told a - gain. It seems the wars will nev - er end.
Dm
C/E
Dm/F
D/F♯
I'll make it home a - gain. I pray you'll fall in love a - gain.
But we'll make it home a - gain, back where we be - long a - gain.
Gm
3fr
Gm7
3fr
F/C
C
Just say you'll en - ter - tain the pos - si - bil - i - ty. I
We're hold - ing on to when we used to dare to dream.

Dm
C/E
Dm/F
D/F♯
learned e - nough from my mis - takes,
learned from all I did - n't say.
We pray we live to see
an - oth - er day in his - to - ry.
Gm
Gm7
G7
F/C
C
Won't you wait for me?
Yes, we still be - lieve.
It

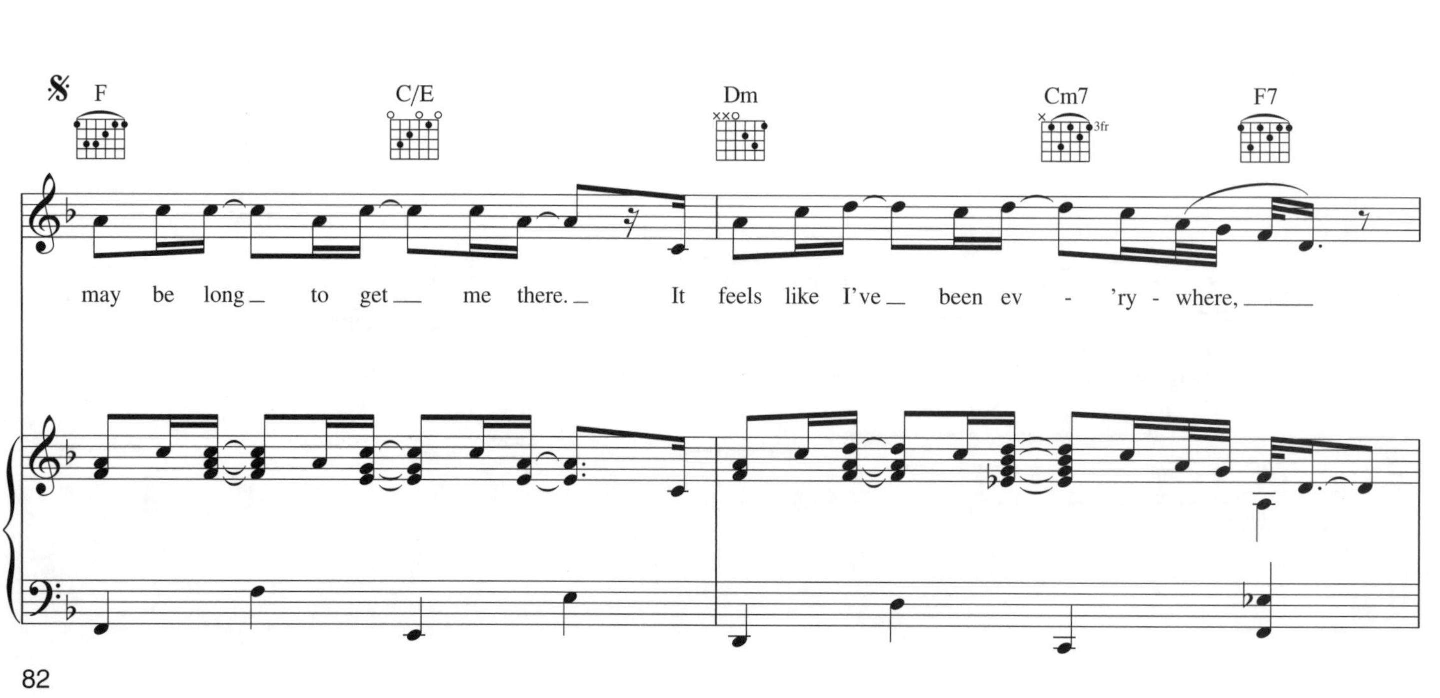
F
C/E
Dm
Cm7
F7
may be long to get me there.
It feels like I've been ev - 'ry - where,

B♭maj7
B♭/C
F
Fsus4
F
but some - day I'll be com - ing home.
C/E
Dm
Cm7
3fr
F7
Round and round the world will spin.
Oh, the cir - cle nev - er ends.
To Coda
1.
2.
B♭maj7
B♭/C
F
Fsus4
F
F
Fsus4
F
So you know that I'll be com - ing home.
Com - ing home,

B♭
F/A
coming home.
Oh.
(I'm coming. I'm coming. I'm coming. I'm coming.
G7
1.
B♭/C
You know that I'll be coming home.
I'm coming. I'm coming. You know that I'll be coming.)
2.
B♭/C
C
Dm
C/E
You know that I'll be coming home.
Oh,
You know that I'll be coming home.)

Dm/F
D/F♯
Gm
3fr
Gm7
3fr
oh, woh, woh.
F/C
C
Dm
C/E
3
I'll be com-ing home. I...
Won't you pray for me.
Dm/F
D/F♯
Gm
3fr
G7
Won't you pray for me.
Yeah,
F/C
C
D.S. al Coda
Coda
Fsus4
F
I'll be com-ing home. It
rit.

great songs series

Cherry Lane Music is proud to present this legendary series which has delighted players and performers for generations.

Great Songs of the Fifties

The latest release in Cherry Lane's acclaimed Great Songs series, this songbook presents 51 musical memories from the fabulous '50s! Features rock, pop, country, Broadway and movie tunes, including: All Shook Up • At the Hop • Blue Suede Shoes • Dream Lover • Fly Me to the Moon • Kansas City • Love Me Tender • Misty • Peggy Sue • Rock Around the Clock • Sea of Love • Sixteen Tons • Take the "A" Train • Wonderful! Wonderful! • and more. Includes an introduction by award-winning journalist Bruce Pollock.

_____02500323 P/V/G............................$16.95

Great Songs of the Sixties, Vol. 1 – Revised Edition

The newly updated version of this classic book includes 80 faves from the 1960s: Angel of the Morning • Bridge over Troubled Water • Cabaret • Different Drum • Do You Believe in Magic • Eve of Destruction • Georgy Girl • It Was a Very Good Year • Monday, Monday • People • Spinning Wheel • Walk on By • and more.

_____02509902 P/V/G............................$19.95

Great Songs of the Sixties, Vol. 2 – Revised Edition

61 more 60s hits: And When I Die • California Dreamin' • Crying • The 59th Street Bridge Song (Feelin' Groovy) • For Once in My Life • Honey • Little Green Apples • MacArthur Park • Me and Bobby McGee • Nowhere Man • Piece of My Heart • Sugar, Sugar • You Made Me So Very Happy • and more.

_____02509904 P/V/G............................$19.95

Great Songs of the Seventies – Revised Edition

This super collection of 70 big hits from the '70s includes: After the Love Has Gone • Afternoon Delight • Annie's Song • Band on the Run • Cold as Ice • FM • Imagine • It's Too Late • Layla • Let It Be • Maggie May • Piano Man • Shelter from the Storm • Superstar • Sweet Baby James • Time in a Bottle • The Way We Were • more!

_____02509917 P/V/G............................$19.95

Prices, contents, and availability subject to change without notice.

Great Songs of the Seventies – Volume 2

Features 58 outstanding '70s songs in rock, pop, country, Broadway and movie genres: American Woman • Baby, I'm-A Want You • Day by Day • Do That to Me One More Time • Dog & Butterfly • Don't Cry Out Loud • Dreamboat Annie • Follow Me • Get Closer • Grease • Heard It in a Love Song • I'll Be There • It's a Heartache • The Loco-Motion • My Eyes Adored You • New Kid in Town • Night Fever • On and On • Sing • Summer Breeze • Tonight's the Night • We Are the Champions • Y.M.C.A. • and more. Includes articles by Cherry Lane Music Company founder Milt Okun, and award-winning music journalist Bruce Pollock.

_____02500322 P/V/G............................$19.95

Great Songs of the Eighties – Revised Edition

This newly revised edition features 50 songs in rock, pop & country styles, plus hits from Broadway and the movies! Songs: Almost Paradise • Angel of the Morning • Do You Really Want to Hurt Me • Endless Love • Flashdance...What a Feeling • Guilty • Hungry Eyes • (Just Like) Starting Over • Let Love Rule • Missing You • Patience • Through the Years • Time After Time • Total Eclipse of the Heart • and more.

_____02502125 P/V/G............................$18.95

Great Songs of the Nineties

This terrific collection features 48 big hits in many styles. Includes: Achy Breaky Heart • Beautiful in My Eyes • Believe • Black Hole Sun • Black Velvet • Blaze of Glory • Building a Mystery • Crash into Me • Fields of Gold • From a Distance • Glycerine • Here and Now • Hold My Hand • I'll Make Love to You • Ironic • Linger • My Heart Will Go On • Waterfalls • Wonderwall • and more.

_____02500040 P/V/G............................$16.95

Great Songs of the Pop Era

Over 50 hits from the pop era, including: Amazed • Annie's Song • Ebony and Ivory • Every Breath You Take • Hey Nineteen • I Want to Know What Love Is • I'm Every Woman • Just the Two of Us • Leaving on a Jet Plane • My Cherie Amour • Raindrops Keep Fallin' on My Head • Rocky Mountain High • This Is the Moment • Time After Time • (I've Had) the Time of My Life • What a Wonderful World • and more!

_____02500043 Easy Piano....................$16.95

6 East 32nd Street, New York, NY 10016

Quality in Printed Music

Visit Cherry Lane on the Internet at
www.cherrylane.com

Exclusively Distributed By

7777 W. Bluemound Rd. P.O. Box 13819 Milwaukee, WI 53213

0402

More Big-Note & Easy Piano Books

For a complete listing of Cherry Lane titles available, including contents listings, please visit our web site at www.cherrylane.com

CLASSICAL CHRISTMAS
Easy solo arrangements of 30 wonderful holiday songs: Ave Maria • Dance of the Sugar Plum Fairy • Evening Prayer • Gesu Bambino • Hallelujah! • He Shall Feed His Flock • March of the Toys • O Come, All Ye Faithful • O Holy Night • Pastoral Symphony • Sheep May Safely Graze • Sinfonia • Waltz of the Flowers • and more.
__02500112 Easy Piano Solo $9.95

BEST OF JOHN DENVER
__02505512 Easy Piano $9.95

DOWN THE AISLE
Easy piano arrangements of 20 beloved pop and classical wedding songs, including: Air on the G String • Ave Maria • Canon in D • Follow Me • Give Me Forever (I Do) • Jesu, Joy of Man's Desiring • Prince of Denmark's March • Through the Years • Trumpet Tune • Unchained Melody • Wedding March • When I Fall in Love • You Decorated My Life • and more.
__025000267 Easy Piano $9.95

EASY BROADWAY SHOWSTOPPERS
Easy piano arrangements of 16 traditional and new Broadway standards, including: "Impossible Dream" from *Man of La Mancha* • "Unusual Way" from *Nine* • "This Is the Moment" from *Jekyll & Hyde* • many more.
__02505517 Easy Piano $12.95

GOLD AND GLORY – THE ROAD TO EL DORADO
This beautiful souvenir songbook features full-color photos and 8 songs from the DreamWorks animated film. Includes original songs by Elton John and Tim Rice, and a score by Hans Zimmer and John Powell. Songs: Cheldorado – Score • El Dorado • Friends Never Say Goodbye • It's Tough to Be a God • Someday out of the Blue (Theme from El Dorado) • The Trail We Blaze • Without Question • Wonders of the New World: To Shibalba.
__02500274 Easy Piano $14.95

A FAMILY CHRISTMAS AROUND THE PIANO
25 songs for hours of family fun, including: Away in a Manger • Deck the Hall • The First Noel • God Rest Ye Merry, Gentlemen • Hark! the Herald Angels Sing • Jingle Bells • Jolly Old St. Nicholas • Joy to the World • O Little Town of Bethlehem • Silent Night, Holy Night • The Twelve Days of Christmas • and more.
__02500398 Easy Piano $7.95

GILBERT & SULLIVAN FOR EASY PIANO
20 great songs from 6 great shows by this beloved duo renowned for their comedic classics. Includes: Behold the Lord High Executioner • The Flowers That Bloom in the Spring • He Is an Englishman • I Am the Captain of the Pinafore • (I'm Called) Little Buttercup • Miya Sama • Three Little Maids • Tit-Willow • We Sail the Ocean Blue • When a Merry Maiden Marries • When Britain Really Ruled the Waves • When Frederic Was a Lad • and more.
__02500270 Easy Piano $12.95

GREAT CONTEMPORARY BALLADS
__02500150 Easy Piano $12.95

HOLY CHRISTMAS CAROLS COLORING BOOK
A terrific songbook with 7 sacred carols and lots of coloring pages for the young pianist. Songs include: Angels We Have Heard on High • The First Noel • Hark! The Herald Angels Sing • It Came upon a Midnight Clear • O Come All Ye Faithful • O Little Town of Bethlehem • Silent Night.
__02500277 Five-Finger Piano $6.95

JEKYLL & HYDE – VOCAL SELECTIONS
Ten songs from the Wildhorn/Bricusse Broadway smash, arranged for big-note: In His Eyes • It's a Dangerous Game • Lost in the Darkness • A New Life • No One Knows Who I Am • Once Upon a Dream • Someone Like You • Sympathy, Tenderness • Take Me as I Am • This Is the Moment.
__02505515 Easy Piano $12.95
__02500023 Big-Note Piano $9.95

JUST FOR KIDS – *NOT!* CHRISTMAS SONGS
This unique collection of 14 Christmas favorites is fun for the whole family! Kids can play the full-sounding big-note solos alone, or with their parents (or teachers) playing accompaniment for the thrill of four-hand piano! Includes: Deck the Halls • Jingle Bells • Silent Night • What Child Is This? • and more.
__02505510 Big-Note Piano $7.95

JUST FOR KIDS – *NOT!* CLASSICS
Features big-note arrangements of classical masterpieces, plus optional accompaniment for adults. Songs: Air on the G String • Dance of the Sugar Plum Fairy • Für Elise • Jesu, Joy of Man's Desiring • Ode to Joy • Pomp and Circumstance • The Sorcerer's Apprentice • William Tell Overture • and more!
__02505513 Classics....................$7.95
__02500301 More Classics $7.95

JUST FOR KIDS – *NOT!* FUN SONGS
Fun favorites for kids everywhere in big-note arrangements for piano, including: Bingo • Eensy Weensy Spider • Farmer in the Dell • Jingle Bells • London Bridge • Pop Goes the Weasel • Puff the Magic Dragon • Skip to My Lou • Twinkle, Twinkle Little Star • and more!
__02505523 Fun Songs................$7.95
__02505528 More Fun Songs $7.95

JUST FOR KIDS – *NOT!* TV THEMES & MOVIE SONGS
Entice the kids to the piano with this delightful collection of songs and themes from movies and TV. These big-note arrangements include themes from The Brady Bunch and The Addams Family, as well as Do-Re-Mi (The Sound of Music), theme from Beetlejuice (Day-O) and Puff the Magic Dragon. Each song includes an accompaniment part for teacher or adult so that the kids can experience the joy of four-hand playing as well! Plus performance tips.
__02505507 TV Themes & Movie Songs $9.95
__02500304 More TV Themes & Movie Songs $9.95

LOVE BALLADS
__02500152 EZ-Play Today #364 $7.95

MERRY CHRISTMAS, EVERYONE
Over 20 contemporary and classic all-time holiday favorites arranged for big-note piano or easy piano. Includes: Away in a Manger • Christmas Like a Lullaby • The First Noel • Joy to the World • The Marvelous Toy • and more.
__02505600 Big-Note Piano $9.95

See your local music dealer or contact:

CHERRY LANE MUSIC COMPANY
6 East 32nd Street, New York, NY 10016

POKEMON 2 B.A. MASTER
This great songbook features easy piano arrangements of 13 tunes from the hit TV series: 2.B.A. Master • Double Trouble (Team Rocket) • Everything Changes • Misty's Song • My Best Friends • Pokémon (Dance Mix) • Pokémon Theme • PokéRAP • The Time Has Come (Pikachu's Goodbye) • Together, Forever • Viridian City • What Kind of Pokémon Are You? • You Can Do It (If You Really Try). Includes a full-color, 8-page pull-out section featuring characters and scenes from this super hot show.
__02500145 Easy Piano $12.95

POKEMON
Five-finger arrangements of 7 songs from the hottest show for kids! Includes: Pokémon Theme • The Time Has Come (Pikachu's Goodbye) • 2B A Master • Together, Forever • What Kind of Pokémon Are You? • You Can Do It (If You Really Try). Also features cool character artwork, and a special section listing the complete lyrics for the "PokéRAP."
__02500291 Five-Finger Piano $7.95

POP/ROCK HITS
__02500153 E-Z Play Today #366$7.95

POP/ROCK LOVE SONGS
Easy arrangements of 18 romatic favorites, including: Always • Bed of Roses • Butterfly Kisses • Follow Me • From This Moment On • Hard Habit to Break • Leaving on a Jet Plane • When You Say Nothing at All • more.
__02500151 Easy Piano $10.95

POPULAR CHRISTMAS CAROLS COLORING BOOK
Kids are sure to love this fun holiday songbook! It features five-finger piano arrangements of seven Christmas classics, complete with coloring pages throughout! Songs include: Deck the Hall • Good King Wenceslas • Jingle Bells • Jolly Old St. Nicholas • O Christmas Tree • Up on the Housetop • We Wish You a Merry Christmas.
__02500276 Five-Finger Piano $6.95

PUFF THE MAGIC DRAGON & 54 OTHER ALL-TIME CHILDREN'S FAVORITE SONGS
55 timeless songs enjoyed by generations of kids, and sure to be favorites for years to come. Songs include: A-Tisket A-Tasket • Alouette • Eensy Weensy Spider • The Farmer in the Dell • I've Been Working on the Railroad • If You're Happy and You Know It • Joy to the World • Michael Finnegan • Oh Where, Oh Where Has My Little Dog Gone • Silent Night • Skip to My Lou • This Old Man • and many more.
__02500017 Big-Note Piano $12.95

PURE ROMANCE
__02500268 Easy Piano $10.95

SCHOOLHOUSE ROCK SONGBOOK
10 unforgettable songs from the classic television educational series, now experiencing a booming resurgence in popularity from Generation X'ers to today's kids! Includes: I'm Just a Bill • Conjunction Junction • Lolly, Lolly, Lolly (Get Your Adverbs Here) • The Great American Melting Pot • and more.
__02505576 Big-Note Piano $8.95

BEST OF JOHN TESH
__02505511 Easy Piano $12.95
__02500128 E-Z Play Today #356$8.95

TOP COUNTRY HITS
__02500154 E-Z Play Today #365$7.95

Prices, contents, and availability subject to change without notice.

More Great Piano/Vocal Books

FROM CHERRY LANE

For a complete listing of Cherry Lane titles available, including contents listings, please visit our web site at
www.cherrylane.com

02500343 Almost Famous $14.95
02502171 The Best of Boston $17.95
02500672 Black Eyed Peas – Elephunk . . . $17.95
02500665 Sammy Cahn Songbook $24.95
02500144 Mary Chapin Carpenter – Party Doll & Other Favorites . . $16.95
02502163 Mary Chapin Carpenter – Stones in the Road $17.95
02502165 John Denver Anthology – Revised $22.95
02502227 John Denver – A Celebration of Life $14.95
02500002 John Denver Christmas $14.95
02502166 John Denver's Greatest Hits $17.95
02502151 John Denver – A Legacy in Song (Softcover) $24.95
02502152 John Denver – A Legacy in Song (Hardcover) $34.95
02500566 Poems, Prayers and Promises: The Art and Soul of John Denver $19.95
02500326 John Denver – The Wildlife Concert $17.95
02500501 John Denver and the Muppets: A Christmas Together $9.95
02509922 The Songs of Bob Dylan $29.95
02500586 Linda Eder – Broadway My Way $14.95
02500497 Linda Eder – Gold $14.95
02500396 Linda Eder – Christmas Stays the Same $17.95
02500175 Linda Eder – It's No Secret Anymore $14.95
02502209 Linda Eder – It's Time $17.95
02500630 Donald Fagen – 5 of the Best . . . $7.95
02500535 Erroll Garner Anthology $19.95
02500270 Gilbert & Sullivan for Easy Piano $12.95
02500318 Gladiator $12.95
02500273 Gold & Glory: The Road to El Dorado $16.95
02502126 Best of Guns N' Roses $17.95
02502072 Guns N' Roses – Selections from Use Your Illusion I and II $17.95
02500014 Sir Roland Hanna Collection . . . $19.95
02500352 Hanson – This Time Around . . . $16.95
02502134 Best of Lenny Kravitz $12.95
02500012 Lenny Kravitz – 5 . . . . $16.95
02500381 Lenny Kravitz – Greatest Hits . . . $14.95
02503701 Man of La Mancha $10.95
02500693 Dave Matthews – Some Devil . . . $16.95
02500555 Dave Matthews Band – Busted Stuff $16.95
02500003 Dave Matthews Band – Before These Crowded Streets $17.95
02502199 Dave Matthews Band – Crash . . $17.95
02500390 Dave Matthews Band – Everyday $14.95
02500493 Dave Matthews Band – Live in Chicago 12/19/98 at the United Center . $14.95
02502192 Dave Matthews Band – Under the Table and Dreaming $17.95
02500681 John Mayer – Heavier Things . . $16.95
02500563 John Mayer – Room for Squares $16.95
02500081 Natalie Merchant – Ophelia $14.95
02500423 Natalie Merchant – Tigerlily . . . $14.95
02502895 Nine $17.95
02500425 Time and Love: The Art and Soul of Laura Nyro $19.95
02502204 The Best of Metallica $17.95
02500407 O-Town $14.95
02500010 Tom Paxton – The Honor of Your Company $17.95
02507962 Peter, Paul & Mary – Holiday Concert $17.95
02500145 Pokemon 2.B.A. Master $12.95
02500026 The Prince of Egypt $16.95
02500660 Best of Bonnie Raitt $17.95
02502189 The Bonnie Raitt Collection $22.95
02502230 Bonnie Raitt – Fundamental . . . $17.95
02502139 Bonnie Raitt – Longing in Their Hearts $16.95
02502088 Bonnie Raitt – Luck of the Draw $14.95
02507958 Bonnie Raitt – Nick of Time . . . $14.95
02502190 Bonnie Raitt – Road Tested $24.95
02502218 Kenny Rogers – The Gift $16.95
02500072 Saving Private Ryan $14.95
02500197 SHeDAISY – The Whole SHeBANG $14.95
02500414 Shrek $14.95
02500536 Spirit – Stallion of the Cimarron $16.95
02500166 Steely Dan – Anthology $17.95
02500622 Steely Dan – Everything Must Go $14.95
02500284 Steely Dan – Two Against Nature $14.95
02500165 Best of Steely Dan $14.95
02500344 Billy Strayhorn: An American Master $17.95
02502132 Barbra Streisand – Back to Broadway $19.95
02500515 Barbra Streisand – Christmas Memories $16.95
02507969 Barbra Streisand – A Collection: Greatest Hits and More $17.95
02502164 Barbra Streisand – The Concert $22.95
02500550 Essential Barbra Streisand $24.95
02502228 Barbra Streisand – Higher Ground $16.95
02500196 Barbra Streisand – A Love Like Ours $16.95
02500280 Barbra Streisand – Timeless . . . $19.95
02503617 John Tesh – Avalon $15.95
02502178 The John Tesh Collection $17.95
02503623 John Tesh – A Family Christmas $15.95
02505511 John Tesh – Favorites for Easy Piano $12.95
02503630 John Tesh – Grand Passion $16.95
02500124 John Tesh – One World $14.95
02500307 John Tesh – Pure Movies 2 . . . . $16.95
02500565 Thoroughly Modern Millie $17.95
02500576 Toto – 5 of the Best $7.95
02502175 Tower of Power – Silver Anniversary $17.95
02502198 The "Weird Al" Yankovic Anthology $17.95
02502217 Trisha Yearwood – A Collection of Hits $16.95
02500334 Maury Yeston – December Songs $17.95
02502225 The Maury Yeston Songbook . . . $19.95

See your local music dealer or contact:

6 East 32nd Street, New York, NY 10016

Quality in Printed Music

EXCLUSIVELY DISTRIBUTED BY

Prices, contents and availability subject to change without notice.
0404